AFTER THE OLYMPICS

TONY MAK

For Nigel Perkins

AFTER THE OLYMPICS

TONY MAK

HOXTON MINI PRESS

INTRODUCTION

Ten years on from the London 2012 Olympic Games, memories of the spectacle have become myths, weaved together as pleasing tapestries of national glory. Competition across 26 sports showcased an apparently clean patriotic meritocracy, while the United Kingdom paraded its history, culture and organisational prowess with a carefully choreographed mixture of irreverence and self-satisfaction: *The Tempest* to the Spice Girls, the NHS to the introduction of women's boxing. Beyond the nostalgia, the physical footprint remains, concentrated on the Olympic Park in Stratford, which reopened to the public the year after the main event. Today, the marvelling crowds have been replaced by jostling shoppers and students. Where there was once athletic competition, battles over legacy and housing now rage. Stratford is a place of hard technicolour edges beside curated parks and starry-eyed start-ups; no different to London's many areas of gentrification, and yet, totally unique.

Development is often sold using optimistic narratives: the promise of better times ahead for existing and future inhabitants, from amenities to investment opportunities. For many of the estimated 590,000 international visitors to the Games, the Olympic Park was an other-worldly, single-use playground – the curves of the stadium, aquatics centre and velodrome providing a futuristic London skyline. For local people, Stratford's post-Olympics transformation was a national prophecy, a promised end to post-industrial neglect ordained by the political and commercial establishments. And yet, its relationship with the Games can feel confused: tenuous homages, obscure redesigns, unequal opportunities. Plans for a 21,000-capacity orb arena featuring the world's largest LED screen have been approved, despite fierce opposition from the local MP and constituents, and the success of the forthcoming East Bank cultural quarter is far from guaranteed. Stratford is still striving for a new purpose: optimising itself for affluent bidders and institutions, but eager to incorporate the Olympic ideals of mass participation and excellence. The aim is to create a sense of inevitability, as if the luxury housing and extravagant entertainment venues were always part of the plan, and have been chosen after a fair and rigorous process. Laying this narrative is as vital for Stratford's success as any concrete foundations.

This is the fractured legacy Tony Mak encountered when he moved to Stratford in 2018 from China. Like many before him, he is an artist attracted to the area for its transport links, shopping and parks. His photographs go in search of Stratford's new purpose, the deeper significance of its cosmetic changes. Armed with old East End maps, Tony followed historic routes including Angel Lane, a market street demolished in 1970, retracing its past and capturing its new guise: a block of 759 rooms for students of King's College London. The whole town has undergone several cycles of boom and bust over the last millennium. Tidal mills on the River Lea supported flour-production in the early Middle Ages, when the region was known for its agriculture. Industrial transition began in the 16th century, when weaving and eventually porcelain joined countless businesses operating in the area. And after Stratford station opened in 1839, locomotive-manufacturing became the major industry for 150 years. In the 20th century, deindustrialisation ushered in decades of disrepair throughout the East End. The successful bid of 2005 promised that the Olympic Park would become a model of social inclusion, offering skills and jobs for people across London and the UK, but especially in the five host boroughs, renamed 'growth boroughs' in anticipation of their rising prospects. While Stratford's facilities and accessibility have doubtless improved, rent hikes in so-called affordable housing have complicated the legacy narrative.

Tony's photographs do not seek to analyse or assess the bid's promises. His is an observational practice, casting a newcomer's inquisitive eye over a town whose future intentionally obscures its past. Cranes loom over polished apartment blocks and the tracks of Stratford station (now the UK's busiest terminal). The River Lea winds through the melee, quietly resolute as its banks are fortified for new infrastructure. There is a feeling of calm, each image seeming to pause the urban tensions which, when they resume, alter the appearance of what has just been captured. There are visual differences between old and new, where material and urban design reveal the layered past. The Olympic Park's greenery is monotonal compared with the Lea Valley's lush vegetation; the steel of luxury blocks pierces the soft brick of abandoned factories. But Tony's presentation is anti-didactic. There is no insistence on utopian harmony, nor does he focus on the irreconcilable visions of what Stratford should be. His subject is spatial reality – life and land as they coexist in individual moments. A neat row of docked hire bikes overlook an office landscape. On a building site, heaps of rubble wait to be transported to relay terrain, powder grey stretching from earth to cloudy sky.

Then there is the emptiness. These photographs were created during and immediately after the UK's first coronavirus lockdown in 2020. The Westfield shopping centre was deserted, as was neighbouring Hackney Wick. Subjects are dwarfed by their surroundings: a lone cyclist outside the velodrome; a boxer and trainer sparring in the shadow of Anish Kapoor's *Orbit* sculpture. There are characters here, but these photographs are urban rather than social documentary. Places largely devoid of people, desertion calling into question architectural function. Tony witnessed Stratford in an altered state, its retail and property machines halted. A new community ethos emerged as locals began to explore their surroundings as recreational rather than commercial spaces. The pandemic interrupted coordinated systems of capital and experience. An organic Olympic legacy by the people took their place.

Tony expresses personal conflict about Stratford's transformation. Growing up in Guangdong, he knows both the damage and opportunities of rapid urban development. Regeneration happens in spite of communities, whether long-standing or recently formed ones. When landscapes and populations change this quickly, photography codifies what memory cannot: not a complete representation of a place's multiplicity, history and conflicts, but a chronicle of its fleeting present. There is one final detail relevant to this project. Were it not for the post-Games development, Tony would not have relocated to Stratford. His is a single, but significant story within the competing choruses of the Olympic legacy. *After the Olympics* is his voice.

Ravi Ghosh
London, 2022

PHOTOGRAPHER'S NOTE

I moved to Stratford in 2018 for the same reasons most people do: it has practical transport links, a convenient shopping centre and the enormous Olympic Park where people flock on the weekends to exercise and relax. But, although I enjoyed the benefits of the area's regeneration, I never really felt I belonged. It was just a place to live where there was nothing much to complain about. And I wasn't the only one who felt that way; to many people, Stratford is just a shiny, soulless suburb on the edge of east London.

Then came the first lockdown in spring 2020. All over the world, we stayed home and waited for the storm outside to pass, observing the changes of time and weather through the only 'viewfinder' we had: our windows. I took a series of photographs from my apartment, overlooking the shopping centre and train station that had brought me there – now standing empty. I started to think about the meaning of 'home' and my own relationship with Stratford, its history and community. When the restrictions eased, I spent months walking around the local area with my camera and old maps of the town centre before its redevelopment; revisiting the venues and new parks and residential developments that sprung up in the wake of the Olympics, as well as the canals and gentrified post-industrial spaces of Hackney Wick. Mostly, I didn't speak to anyone. I stood from a distance and observed. As an 'outsider', taking pictures was my attempt to engage with my surroundings and, in doing so, I discovered unknown places and saw many unexpected aspects of Stratford. After living there for two years, I finally started to pay attention to my neighborhood.

The more I saw of Stratford, the more I understood that the amenities that drew me to the area came with a price. Ten years after the Olympics, the regeneration of Stratford is still ongoing and the gap between wealthier newcomers and the established community continues to widen. The changes here have not served everyone equally. But at a time when our attention is dominated by online feeds, it's easy to neglect the neighborhood we actually live in. Perhaps it's time for us to pay more attention, and, in doing so, try to make our local areas better for everyone.

Tony Mak
Guangdong, 2022

IMAGE CAPTIONS

p9	River Lea wetlands, 2020
p11	Stratford Town Centre Link, 2020
p12	Stratford International station, 2020
p15	Meridian Square, 2020
p17	Queen Elizabeth Olympic Park, 2020
p19	Near Stratford High Street station, 2020
p21	Lee Valley VeloPark, 2020
p23	Wallis Road, Hackney Wick, 2020
p24	A106, near Hackney Marshes, 2020
p27	Lee Navigation, 2020
p29	Sugar House Island, 2020
p31	Queen Elizabeth Olympic Park, 2020
p33	Sugar House Island, 2020
p35	Near London Aquatic Centre, 2020
p37	Hackney Marshes, 2020
p39	Pudding Mill Lane station, 2020
p40	UCL East construction site, 2020
p43	Lee Valley Hockey and Tennis Centre, 2020
p45	St Thomas Creek Footbridge, 2020
p49	Great Eastern Road, near Stratford Centre, 2020
p50	Bank of River Lea, 2020
p51	Fish Island Village, 2020
p53	Queen Elizabeth Olympic Park, 2020
p55	Meridian Square, 2020
p57	Queen Elizabeth Olympic Park, 2020
p59	Endeavour Square, 2020
p60	East Bank, 2020
p63	River Lea, near Bow Roundabout, 2020

p65	Channelsea River, near Three Mills Lock, 2020	p97	Waterworks River, 2020
p67	Sugar House Island, 2020	p99	Lee Valley VeloPark, 2021
p69	Hertford Union Canal, 2020	p101	River Lea wetlands, 2021
p73	White Post Lane, Hackney Wick, 2020	p102	River Lea, 2020
p75	Near London Aquatic Centre, 2020	p105	River Lea, near Bow Roundabout, 2020
p77	Queen Elizabeth Olympic Park, 2020	p106	Salway Place, 2020
p79	Near Marshgate Lane, 2020	p109	Victory Park, East Village, 2020
p80	Kennard Road, near Stratford station, 2020	p110	Weavers Row, near East Village, 2020
p83	High Street, near Marshgate Lane, 2020	p113	Honour Lea Avenue, East Village, 2020
p85	River Lea wetlands, 2020	p117	Stratford station, 2020
p87	Queen Elizabeth Olympic Park, 2020	p118	Coopers Lane, near East Village, 2020
p91	Near Stratford Centre, 2020		
p93	Near Old Ford Lock, 2020		
p94	Westfield Avenue, 2020		

After the Olympics

First edition, published 2022
by Hoxton Mini Press, London

Book design copyright © Hoxton Mini Press 2022
All photographs by Tony Mak
Introduction by Ravi Ghosh
Design and sequence by Friederike Huber
Additional design by Richard Mason
Copy-editing by Octavia Stocker
Production by Sarah-Louise Deazley
All rights reserved

No part of this publication may be reproduced, stored in a retrieval system, or transmitted in any form or by any means, electronic, mechanical, photocopying, recording or otherwise, without the prior written permission of the copyright owner.

ISBN: 978-1-914314-27-8

A CIP catalogue record for this book is available from the British Library.

Printed and bound by OZGraf, Poland

Hoxton Mini Press is an environmentally conscious publisher, committed to offsetting our carbon footprint. The offset for this book was purchased from Stand For Trees.

For every book you buy from our website, we plant a tree:
www.hoxtonminipress.com